Great Earth Science Projects™

Hands-on Projects About
Rocks, Minerals, and Fossils

Krista West

The Rosen Publishing Group's
PowerKids Press™
New York

Some of the projects in this book were designed for a child to do together with an adult.

Published in 2002 by The Rosen Publishing Group, Inc.
29 East 21st Street, New York, NY 10010

First Edition

Book Design: Michael de Guzman
Project Editor: Jennifer Quasha, Jason Moring, Jennifer Landau

Photo Credits: p. 4 (top left) (igneous rock) © Scott T. Smith/CORBIS; p. 4, (top right) (sedimentary rock) © David Muench/CORBIS; p. 4 (botttom left) (metamorphic rock) © Richard Hamilton Smith/CORBIS; p. 4 (bottom right) (fossil) © Lester V. Bergman/CORBIS; pp. 6–21 by Cindy Reiman.

West, Krista.
    Hands-on projects about rocks, minerals, and fossils / Krista West.—1st ed.
        p. cm.— (Great earth science projects)
    Includes index.
    ISBN 0-8239-5842-6 (lib. bdg.)
    1. Rocks—Experiments—Juvenile literature. 2. Minerals—Experiments—Juvenile literature. 3. Fossils—Experiments—Juvenile literature. [1. Rocks. 2. Minerals. 3. Fossils.] I. Title. II. Series.

QE432.2 W35 2002
550'.78—dc21   00-011691

Manufactured in the United States of America

Contents

How Rocks, Minerals, and Fossils Are Formed

Minerals are natural ingredients that make up almost everything on the planet. Mixtures of minerals that have been heated, squeezed, cooled, or hardened by Earth are called rocks. Scientists **classify** rocks according to how they were formed. A mixture of hot, liquid minerals from underground that has been cooled and hardened forms **igneous rocks**, such as the Earth's **crust**. Layers of minerals that have been cemented together by natural forces form **sedimentary rocks** such as limestone, sandstone, and shale. Minerals or other rocks that have been heated and squeezed inside Earth form **metamorphic rocks**, such as marble, gneiss, and schist. **Fossils** are the remains of living things that have left an **impression**, or print, in rock or that have turned into rock over time.

← *Clockwise from top left are examples of igneous rocks, sedimentary rocks, fossils, and metamorphic rocks.*

Find Minerals in Your Home

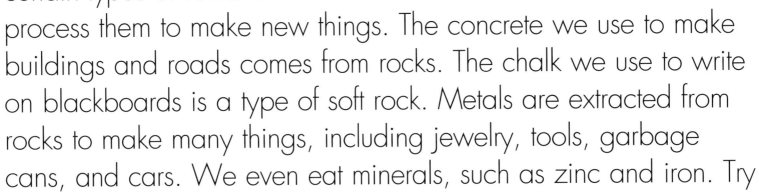

You may not realize it, but we use things made from rocks and minerals every day. Often we take certain types of rocks and minerals from Earth and process them to make new things. The concrete we use to make buildings and roads comes from rocks. The chalk we use to write on blackboards is a type of soft rock. Metals are extracted from rocks to make many things, including jewelry, tools, garbage cans, and cars. We even eat minerals, such as zinc and iron. Try to find some of these objects in your home and figure out what minerals they contain.

You will need

- A pencil
- A piece of paper
- Various household objects

1 Divide a piece of paper in half. List these common objects down the left side of the page:

salt
pencil
glass
ceramic pot
jewelry
penny

2 Walk around your house and try to find the objects listed on your page. Put a check mark next to the ones you see.

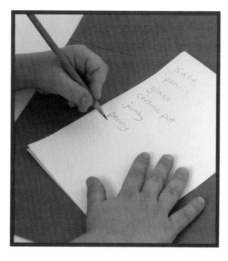

3 All of these objects are made of minerals. On the right side of the page, try to guess what mineral the object contains.

4 Compare your answers to the chart below. Are you surprised?

Object	Mineral
salt	Salt is a mineral.
pencil	Lead is a soft rock.
glass	Glass is made from sand, a mixture of tiny nonmetallic minerals.
ceramic pot	Ceramic is made from clay, a nonmetallic mineral.
jewelry	Gemstones, such as diamonds, rubies, and sapphires, are rocks. Gold and silver are minerals.
penny	Pennies are zinc coated with copper, a metallic mineral.

Make "Igneous Rock" Candy

Igneous rocks are formed when a mixture of hot, liquid minerals cools and hardens. The mixture of hot, liquid minerals inside Earth is called **magma**. When magma reaches Earth's surface, it is called **lava**. Volcanoes are places where lava reaches the surface of Earth and cools to form igneous rocks. In the United States, the land near recently active volcanoes is made almost entirely of **basalt**, a type of igneous rock. Although we aren't going to make an igneous rock, we can make a similar substance by using food found in the kitchen.

You will need

- 5 ounces (142 g) of evaporated milk
- 2 cups (448 g) of sugar
- 12 ounces (340 g) of chocolate chips
- A large casserole dish
- Waxed paper to line the casserole dish
- A pot
- A stovetop burner

8

1 In the pot, heat the milk until it is warm. Add the sugar and stir until it dissolves. Then slowly add the chocolate chips and stir until you have a thick liquid. This hot liquid is similar to the hot, liquid minerals that eventually turn into magma.

2 Pour the mixture into a casserole dish lined with waxed paper. The mixture spreads in the dish just like lava spreads over Earth.

3 Put the dish with the mixture in the refrigerator overnight. In the morning, the liquid will have cooled and hardened. This hardening process is similar to what happens to real magma and lava as they cool and harden into igneous rock.

Create a Sedimentary Rock

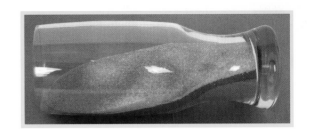

A **sediment** is a tiny mineral that has broken off an exposed landform such as a mountain or a hillside. Wind and water often pick up and move sediments to new locations. Sediments wash into lakes, rivers, and oceans and settle at the bottom of the water. Over time, the sediment is cemented into a layer of minerals. Gradually more sediments wash into the water and settle, forming a new layer on top of the old layer. As the layers are squeezed and hardened, they become sedimentary rock. The same process can happen on land. Minerals are deposited in layers by wind or water and then form sedimentary rocks. You can create the beginnings of a sedimentary rock at home using sand and salt.

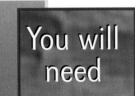

You will need

- Three colors of sand
- Salt
- An 8-ounce (23-cl) glass

Pour about half an inch (13 mm) of sand in the bottom of the glass. Sand is made of quartz, a clear, hard mineral, and other minerals. This is your first layer of minerals.

Now add a layer of salt, which is another mineral. Repeat steps 1 and 2 until you have many layers of minerals.

If you let the layers squeeze together, either underwater or on Earth, in time they would harden into sedimentary rock. Layers of sand aren't always straight and flat. Empty your glass and make some new layers. This time, try tilting the glass after each layer and see what happens to your layers.

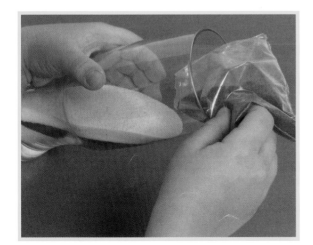

Make a Metamorphic Rock Replica

Rocks that are heated and then squeezed deep inside Earth are called metamorphic rocks. Any type of rock—an igneous rock, sedimentary rock, or even a metamorphic rock—can be heated and squeezed to become a new metamorphic rock. You can find metamorphic rocks near mountains, where Earth pushes up existing rocks. During the mountain-making process, the existing rocks are heated and reshaped into metamorphic rocks. In your kitchen, you can copy the process metamorphic rocks go through with clay, a nonmetallic mineral.

You will need

- Blue clay that can be baked
- Yellow clay that can be baked
- A 12-inch (30.5-cm) piece of string
- A cookie sheet
- An oven

1 Have an adult help you preheat the oven to the heat shown on the package.

2 Think of each color of clay as a different type of mineral. Mix your minerals together to make a ball. The mixing represents the reshaping and squeezing that happens to rocks deep inside Earth. Be careful not to mix them too much because you will want to be able to see both colors.

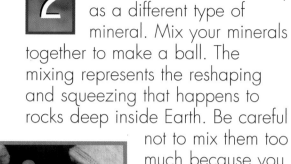

3 Take one end of the string in one hand and hold it tightly. Then take the other end of the string in your other hand and hold it tightly. Now stretch the string between your hands, press it through the middle of the ball of clay, and slice it in half. This gives you a better view of the inside of your "metamorphic rock."

4 Place the two pieces of clay on a cookie sheet and bake them as directed in the instructions on the package. The heat from the oven represents the heat from deep inside Earth. Remove the cookie sheet and let it cool. The clay minerals should have hardened into a substance like a metamorphic rock. Can you make other kinds? What might a mountain made of metamorphic rocks look like?

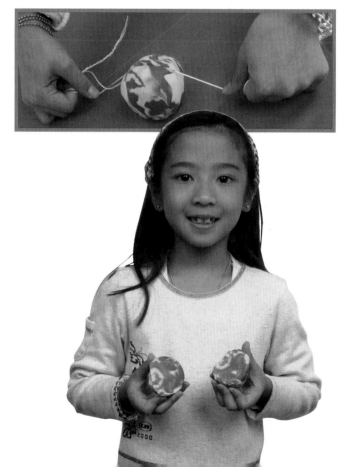

Classify Rocks and Minerals by Their Hardness

Scientists identify rocks and minerals by examining their **properties**, such as color, streak, **density**, and hardness. Scientists rate the hardness of minerals on the **Mohs scale**. The Mohs scale ranges from 1 to 10. One is the softest rating and 10 is the hardest. Your fingernail's hardness is between 2 and 3. A nail made of steel has a hardness rating between 6 and 7. The next project in this book is like a **streak test**. Can you rate the hardness of objects in your home?

You will need

- Your fingernail
- A steel nail
- A piece of paper
- A pencil
- Chalk
- A glass jar
- A copper penny

1 Things to test:
Chalk (limestone, a sedimentary rock)
A copper penny
A lead pencil
A glass soda bottle or jam jar
Sandpaper

On a piece of paper, write the numbers from 1 to 10, leaving a lot of space to write between the numbers. This is your hardness scale. Halfway between 2 and 3, write "fingernail," and halfway between 6 and 7, write "nail."

2 Now pick up the penny and scratch your fingernail. If there is a scratch mark on your fingernail, it means your fingernail is softer than copper. If there isn't a scratch, your fingernail is harder than copper. Write "penny" on your hardness scale wherever it falls, either above or below "fingernail."

3 Next scratch the penny with the nail. Does the nail scratch the penny? Check your hardness scale again. Is your penny in the right place on the scale?

4 Try scratching each of your objects first with your fingernail and then with the nail. Write their names on the hardness scale where you think they should be placed. To get a really good scale, try comparing the objects with each other. Does the penny scratch the glass? How about the sandpaper?

Start a Batch of Coal

Did you know that **coal** is made from plant fossils? Coal is the remains of leaves, bark, and wood that were smashed and hardened over time between layers of sedimentary rock. Coal forms when the plant remains are trapped in a place where there isn't much oxygen. In such an environment, bacteria use the oxygen and hydrogen from the plant, leaving behind carbon. If the area is covered by layers of sediment, the carbon is trapped in sedimentary rock layers. Over time, the carbon turns into coal. We take coal from the sedimentary rock and burn it to create energy. You can begin a batch of coal at home.

You will need

- A clear glass jar
- Five crushed leaves
- Five small sticks
- One cup of dirt
- One cup of sand
- Pebbles

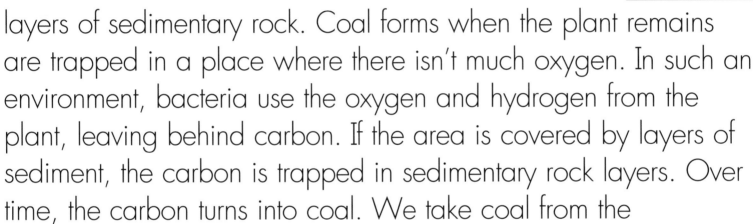

1 Fill the bottom of your jar with one inch (25 mm) of pebbles.

 2 Sprinkle the leaves and sticks on top of the pebbles.

 3 Cover with a one-inch (25-mm) layer of dirt. Then add a layer of sand. Repeat steps 1 through 3 so you have two layers of everything.

 4 You now have the beginnings of a sedimentary rock containing coal. If your rock got buried for millions of years and had pressure put on it, the leaves and sticks would turn to coal and would be separated by layers of rock.

Make a Fossil-like Impression

Fossils are the remains of ancient creatures that are preserved in rock. Fossils can be impressions from hard objects such as bones, shells, or wood, or soft things such as leaves, feathers, or footprints. Fossils form when living things die or make a mark on soft layers such as mud or sand. When the layers harden and become rocks, they sometimes keep the shape of the object. Soft sediments also can harden around an object and create a solid mold. When the object breaks down, minerals fill the space and harden into rocks of the same shape. You can make a fossil-like impression yourself.

You will need

- A mixing bowl
- Clay
- Nonstick cooking spray
- A small, hard object such as a pinecone or a coin

1 Spread a layer of clay in the bottom of a bowl. This is your soft sediment layer.

2 Spray the surface with the cooking spray.

3 Lay your object on the surface of the clay and press down gently to make an impression. The object is like the ancient creature leaving its mark.

4 Lift up the object and let the clay harden. You've made a fossil!

Go on a Fossil Hunt

Are there fossils hiding in your neighborhood? Take a look! Observation, or looking, is the first skill you need to find fossils. Scientists use observation to learn about new things. They draw pictures or write about what they see. After observing, scientists try to explain what they saw. With fossils, they might ask questions such as what creature formed the fossil? When was it formed? How was it formed? Go on a fossil hunt in your neighborhood but approach it like a scientist. How many fossils can you find?

You will need
- A pad of paper
- A pencil
- A magnifying glass

1 Take a walk through your neighborhood. Ask an adult to go with you because some fossils are hard to find.

2 If you see a sidewalk, look closely at it. Do you see any places where people or animals walked in the cement before it was dry? These are modern fossils. Write and draw what you see in your notebook.

3 Do you see any large rocks or boulders? Examine them closely with a magnifying glass for marks. Can you find any impressions or scratches? These could be fossils, too. Record what you see.

4 Look for animal tracks, impressions of leaves on the ground, or other fossils. Record what you find in your notebook.

Use What You've Learned

Now that you have learned about rocks, minerals, and fossils, think about the world in which you live. On the way to school, see how many rocks and minerals you can spot. Next time you go to the park or the beach, search for fossils. Challenge your friends and see who can find the most fossils. Rocks, minerals, and fossils are all around us every day. We just have to know what to look for. It doesn't take much time and the more you look, the more you'll learn.

Glossary

basalt (buh-SALT) A hard, dark-colored igneous rock found in Earth's crust.

classify (KLA-seh-fy) To arrange in groups.

coal (KOHL) The remains of leaves, bark, and wood smashed and hardened over time between layers of sedimentary rock.

crust (KRUST) The outer layer of Earth.

density (DEN-seh-tee) The heaviness of an object compared to its size.

fossils (FAH-sulz) The hardened remains of a dead animal or plant that lived long ago.

igneous rocks (IG-nee-us ROX) Hot liquid minerals from underground that have cooled and hardened.

impression (im-PREH-shen) A print made by pushing on soft material.

lava (LAH-vuh) Magma that has reached the surface of Earth.

magma (MAG-muh) Hot, liquid minerals inside Earth.

metamorphic rocks (meh-tuh-MOR-fik ROX) Minerals or rocks that have been heated and squeezed inside Earth.

minerals (MIH-ner-ulz) The natural ingredients that make up almost everything on Earth.

Mohs scale (MOHZ SKAYL) A hardness scale for rocks and minerals, used by scientists.

properties (PRAH-pur-teez) Characteristics or qualities.

sediment (SED-ih-ment) Tiny pieces of minerals that have been broken off mountains, hillsides, or other exposed landforms.

sedimentary rocks (sed-ih-MEN-teh-ree ROX) Layers of minerals that have been squeezed.

streak test (STREEK TEST) A method used by scientists to help identify rocks and minerals.

Index

Web Sites

To learn more about rocks, minerals, and fossils, check out these Web sites:

http://pubs.usgs.gov/gip/acidrain/contents.html
http://walrus.wr.usgs.gov/ask-a-geologist/